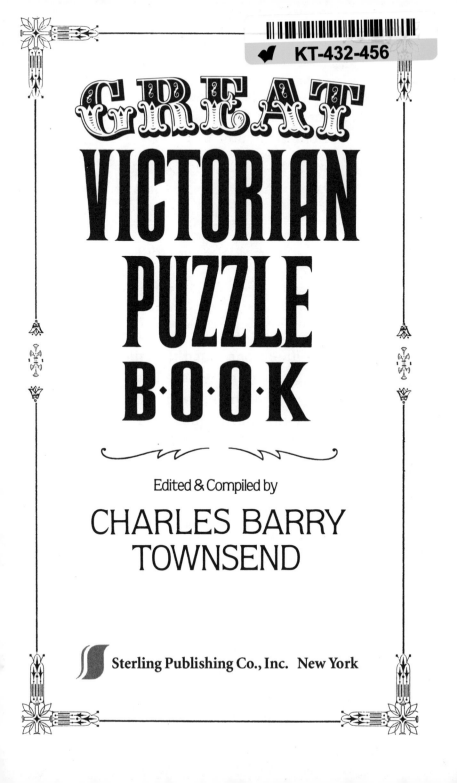

GREAT
VICTORIAN
PUZZLE
B·O·O·K

Edited & Compiled by

CHARLES BARRY
TOWNSEND

Sterling Publishing Co., Inc. New York

This book is dedicated to the memory of two distinguished Princeton Tigers, one from the North and one from the South:

Charles Howard Townsend, Class of 1919
Harold Calhoun Smith, Class of 1935

Library of Congress Cataloging-in-Publication Data

Townsend, Charles Barry.
  Great Victorian puzzle book / compiled and edited by Charles Barry
Townsend.
    p.   cm.
  Selection of items from Louis Hoffmann's Puzzles old and new, 1893.
  Includes index.
  ISBN 0-8069-0388-0
  1. Puzzles.   2. Puzzles—History—19th century.   I. Hoffmann,
Louis, 1839–1919. Puzzles old and new.   II. Title.
  GV1493.T67   1993
  793.73—dc20   93-22700
                                                                    CIP

10   9   8   7   6   5   4   3   2   1

Published by Sterling Publishing Company, Inc.
387 Park Avenue South, New York, N.Y. 10016
© 1993 by Charles Barry Townsend
Distributed in Canada by Sterling Publishing
% Canadian Manda Group, P.O. Box 920, Station U
Toronto, Ontario, Canada M8Z 5P9
Distributed in Great Britain and Europe by Cassell PLC
Villiers House, 41/47 Strand, London WC2N 5JE, England
Distributed in Australia by Capricorn Link Ltd.
P.O. Box 665, Lane Cove, NSW 2066
Manufactured in the United States of America

Sterling ISBN 0-8069-0388-0

Contents

Introduction

Exactly one hundred years ago, in 1893, a milestone in puzzle literature was reached in England. The father of modern magical literature, Professor Louis Hoffmann, took time out from cataloging the wonders of the Victorian stage conjurers to write a book dealing with the best puzzles of his day. The book contained over 400 pages and described hundreds of problems. Besides presenting conundrums dealing with coins and matches, words and mathematics, the professor also explained the workings of a variety of mechanical puzzles, many of which are still available today. To make sure that everything was crystal-clear, Professor Hoffmann added hundreds of engravings to the collection.

This great book, which certainly ranks with the collected works of Sam Loyd and H. E. Dudeney, has, for too long, been absent from the shelves of booksellers. *Great Victorian Puzzle Book* presents readers with some of the choicest items from Professor Hoffmann's classic work. In the future we intend to offer a second helping of these Victorian delights. So now settle back and prepare to start a most enjoyable and puzzling journey into the past.

Your editor,
Charles Barry Townsend

Preface to the 1893 Edition of *Puzzles Old and New*

The Natural History of the Puzzle has yet to be written. It is a plant of very ancient growth, as witness the riddle of the Sphinx, solved by Edipus, and the enigma wherewith Samson confounded his Philistine adversaries. Homer is said by Plutarch to have died of chagrin at being unable to guess a riddle; and folklore abounds in instances where the winning of a princess, or the issue of some perilous adventure, is made to depend upon success in solving some puzzle, verbal or otherwise. In more modern times grave mathematicians, like Cardan and Euler, have not disdained to employ their leisure in the fabrication of "posers" for the puzzlement of their less erudite compeers.

The chief difficulties I have found in compiling the present collection have been nomenclature and classification. In view of the varieties of taste, some preferring a mathematical, some a mechanical problem—it seemed desirable to have as many categories as possible. On the other hand, the more numerous the divisions, the more difficult does it become to assign a given puzzle definitely to one or another. In many instances the same item might with equal propriety be classed under either of several categories.

Nomenclature presents even greater difficulties. The same title is often applied, with more or less appropriateness, to two or three different puzzles. For example, there are some half-dozen "cross" puzzles, more or less unlike, yet all having a fair claim to the title, and being scarcely distinguishable by any other. Again, a mechanical puzzle is frequently described in the price-lists of different dealers by different names, the "Arabian Mystery" of one being, say, the "Egyptian Paradox" or the "Ashantee Difficulty" of another. Others are of necessity nameless, it being impossible to devise any short title which shall give any idea of the nature of the problem.

The very wide class of verbal puzzles, comprising conundrums, enigmas, charades, etc., is here, from considerations of space, omitted. With this exception, it has been my endeavour to make this little book as complete as possible, and I have to acknowledge a substantial debt of thanks to the many friends (notably Messrs. Paul Perkins and Edward Montauban) who have lent helping hands to make it so. The field is, however, very wide, and it is almost a matter of course that many "good things" should have been, through ignorance or inadvertence, omitted. Should any reader note such omissions, or have private information as to items of special merit, I shall be glad, with a view to future editions, to be made acquainted with them.

Louis Hoffmann
Puzzles Old and New

1
Puzzles With Counters

Puzzles of this class are frequently propounded in more or less fanciful forms, *e.g.*, a gardener is required to plant trees, or an officer to place troops, in such manner as to answer the conditions of the problem. From considerations of space, we leave such fanciful elaborations for the most part to the imagination of the reader. Readers who prefer to put any question in such a shape will have little difficulty in inventing an appropriate legend.

Problem Using Eleven Counters

Required, to arrange eleven counters in such manner that they shall form twelve rows, with three counters in each row.

Problem Using Nine Counters

Required, to arrange nine counters in such manner that they shall form ten rows, with three counters in each row.

Problem Using Twenty-Seven Counters

Required, to arrange twenty-seven counters in such manner as to form nine rows, with six counters in each row.

Problem Using Ten Counters

Required, to arrange ten counters in such manner that they shall form five rows, with four counters in each row.

Another Problem Using Ten Counters

Required, to place ten counters so they shall count four in a row in eight different directions.

Problem Using Nineteen Counters

Required, to arrange nineteen counters in such manner that they shall form nine rows of five counters each.

The Monastery Problem

Given, a square, divided into nine smaller squares. Required, to arrange counters in the eight outer squares in such manner that there shall always be nine on each side of the square, though the total be repeatedly varied, being 24, 20, 28, 32, and 36 in succession.

This is a very ancient problem. It is usually propounded after the fashion following: A blind abbot was at the head of a monastery of twenty-four monks, who were domiciled three in a cell in eight cells, occupying the four sides of a square, while the abbot himself occupied a cell in the middle. To assure himself that all were duly housed for the night, he was in the habit of visiting the cells at frequent intervals and counting the occupants, reckoning that if he found nine monks in each row of three cells, the tale was complete.

But the brethren succeeded in eluding his vigilance. First, four of them absented themselves (reducing the number to twenty), but still the abbot counted and found nine in a row. Then these four returned, bringing four friends with them, thus making twenty-eight

12

persons, and yet the normal nine in a row was not increased. Presently four more outsiders came in, making thirty-two. The result was the same. Again, four more visitors arrived, making a total of thirty-six, but the abbot, going his rounds, found nine persons in each row as before.

How was this managed?

The Eight-Pointed Star Problem

This is a puzzle of a different character.

Given, an eight-pointed star, as shown here, and seven counters. You are required to place the counters on seven of the points of the star, in so doing strictly following this rule: Each counter is to be drawn from a vacant point along the corresponding line to another vacant point, and there left. You then start from another vacant point, and proceed in like manner till the seven points are covered.

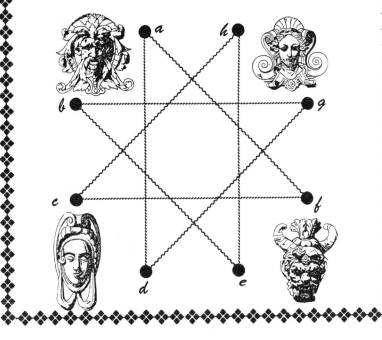

The "Crowning" Puzzle

This is sometimes known as the "crowning" puzzle. The reader will remember that at the game of checkers a piece reaching the opposite side of the board becomes a king, and is "crowned" by having a second piece placed on the top of it. In the case of this puzzle, ten counters, or pieces, are placed in a row, and the player is required to "crown" five of them after the following fashion: Take up one counter, pass it to the right or left *over two others*, and crown the one next in order, proceeding in like manner till the whole are crowned.

A king, it should be stated, is still regarded as being *two* counters.

An Intersection Problem

Given, the figure shown below.

Required, to place at the intersections of its various lines twenty-one counters, in such manner as to form thirty rows of three counters each, each group of three being united by one of the lines.

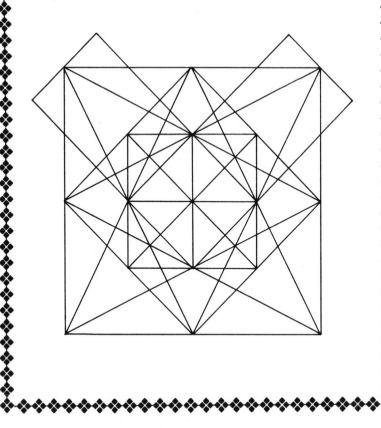

The "Right and Left" Puzzle

This is a very excellent puzzle, and has the special recommendation of being very little known. Rule on cardboard a rectangular figure consisting of seven equal spaces, each one inch square. In the three spaces to the left place three red, and in the three spaces to the right three white counters, the space in the middle being left unoccupied.

The puzzle is to transpose the red and white counters, so that the three white shall be in the left-hand, and the three red in the right-hand spaces. This is to be done according to the following rules:

1. Each counter can only be moved one space at a time.

2. If a counter is divided from a vacant space by one single counter only, it may pass over it into such vacant space.

3. Counters may only be moved in a *forward* direction—i.e., red to the right, and white to the left. A move once made cannot be retracted.

Another "Right and Left" Puzzle

This is a further development of the same problem. Rule a sheet of paper into squares so that each horizontal row shall contain seven, and each vertical row five, and upon them place red and white counters (17 of each color), as shown below. Leave the central space (No. 18) vacant.

You are required, under the same conditions as in the last case, to transpose the red and white counters.

The "Four and Four" Puzzle

This is very similar to the two "Right and Left" puzzles, but is worked out differently.

Rule on cardboard a rectangular figure, divide it into ten squares, and in the first eight spaces, beginning from the left hand, dispose eight counters, red and black alternately.

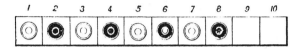

The puzzle is, moving them *two at a time*, to get the four red and the four black counters grouped each color together without any space between them. This must be done *in four moves only*. At the close of the operation the eight counters should be as shown below.

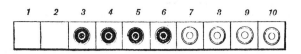

They are then to be worked back again, after the same fashion, to their original positions.

The "English Sixteen" Puzzle

A clever puzzle, under the above title, is issued by Messrs. Heywood, of Manchester, England. In the result to be attained it is almost identical with "Another 'Right and Left' Puzzle," but the conditions are somewhat different and the puzzle considerably more difficult.

A board, as illustrated below, is used, with eight white and eight red counters. These are arranged on the *black* squares, the red to the right, the white to the left, the central square, No. 9 in the figure, left vacant. The problem is to transpose the red and white counters, moving the pieces according to "checkers" rules, *i.e.*, forward only; the whites towards the spaces occupied by the reds, and the reds towards the spaces occupied by the whites. The pieces move only on the black squares, and therefore diagonally. A white piece can pass over a black one, and a black piece over a white one, provided the next space is vacant.

Puzzles With Matchsticks

There are many puzzles, of various degrees of merit, performed with the aid of matchsticks. Here is a brief selection.

Problem Using Eleven Matches

Take eleven matches. Arrange them to make nine of them.

Problem Using Nine Matches

Take nine matches. Arrange them to make three dozen.

A Triangle Puzzle

Using six matches, form four triangles of equal size.

A Bridge of Matches

Take three wine glasses and three matches. Using the three matches, form a bridge between the three wine glasses strong enough to support a fourth wine glass.

Note: Each match must rest on one glass only and touch it only at a single point.

A Match Square Problem

Arrange twenty-four matches on the table to form nine squares, as shown below. Now, take away eight matches and leave two squares only.

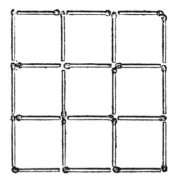

The Seventeen Match Puzzle

Place seventeen matches on the table to form six equal squares, as shown below. Take away five matches and leave three squares only.

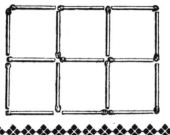

Another Seventeen Match Puzzle

Arrange seventeen matches on the table to form six equal squares as in the "Seventeen Match Puzzle." Now, take away six matches to leave two squares only.

The Fifteen Matches Puzzle

This is a game, but it may also be presented as a puzzle.

Fifteen matchsticks (or counters) are placed side by side on the table. One player takes one end of the row, the other player the other. Each in turn removes up to three matchsticks.

The object is to avoid being the one to remove the last match. To all appearances, this is a game of chance, but a player who knows the secret can always compel a novice adversary to take the last piece.

How is this done?

A Match-Shifting Problem

Place twelve matches on the table to form four equal squares, as shown below. Remove and replace four matches to form exactly three squares, each the same size as the first four.

Another Match-Shifting Problem

Arrange fifteen matches on the table to form five equal squares, as shown below. Remove three matches so that three such squares only remain.

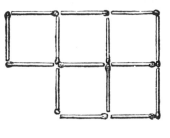

An Uplifting Puzzle

Four matches are used in this puzzle. With a sharp penknife split the upper end of one of them to form a notch, and pare the end of another to a wedge shape. Insert the wedge into the notch, so that the two matches shall form an angle of about 60°. With these two and a third match, placed to lean against the point where the two meet, form a tripod on the table, as shown below.

The puzzle is to lift these three simultaneously with the end of the fourth match using only one hand.

3

"Quibble" or "Catch" Puzzles

The present chapter is devoted to puzzles that depend on a double meaning or an unnatural interpretation of the question, which then assumes a second, less obvious significance.

Subtraction Extraordinary

Required, to take one from nineteen and leave twenty.

How is it to be done?

A New Way of Writing 100

Required, to express 100 by repetition of the same figure six times over.

Two Halves Greater Than the Whole

Prove that seven is the half of twelve.

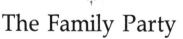

The Family Party

A family gathering included one grandfather, one grandmother, two fathers, two mothers, four children, three grandchildren, one brother, two sisters, two sons, two daughters, one father-in-law, one mother-in-law, and one daughter-in-law, and yet there were only seven persons present.

How can the two statements be reconciled?

The Flying Coin

Place a coin in each hand and extend your arms shoulder high. Now, bring both coins into one hand without allowing your arms to approach each other.

Three Times Six

Place three sixes together to make seven.

A Queer Query

Twice ten are six of us,
Six are but three of us,
Nine are but four of us;
   What can we possibly be?
Would you know more of us,
Twelve are but six of us,
   Five are but four, do you see?

Multiplication Extraordinary

What three figures, multiplied by five, will make six?

The Last Thing Out

You undertake to show another person something which you never saw before, which he never saw before, and which, after you both have seen, no one else will ever see again.

How is it to be done?

The Mysterious Addition

1. I add one to five, and make it four. How can that be?
2. What must I add to nine to make it six?

The Three Gingerbread Nuts

This is propounded in the shape of a magic trick, usually after two or three bona fide tricks have been performed. Place three gingerbread nuts on the table and cover each with a borrowed hat. (In default of gingerbread nuts, three almonds, raisins, or any other small edible articles may be substituted.) Making a great point of having nothing concealed in your hands, profess your willingness to allow the audience, if they please, to mark the three articles, so that there can be no question of substitution.

Then, take up each hat in succession, pick up the nut (or its substitute) beneath it, and gravely eat it, replacing the hat mouth downwards on the table. Anyone is at liberty to see that there is nothing left under either hat. Finally, undertake to bring the three nuts under whichever of the three hats the company may select; and the choice being made, at once do so.

How is it to be done?

Magic Made Easy

Borrow two coins of different sizes and hold them one in each hand, with your hands open and in front of you, about two feet apart. Now close your hands, and announce that you will make the coins change places without again opening your hands, and do just what you said you would.

How is it done?

MORE "QUIBBLE"
AND "CATCH"
QUESTIONS BY
PROFESSOR
HOFFMANN

The Portrait

A portrait hung in a gentleman's library. He was asked whom it represented. He replied,
   "Uncles and brothers have I none,
   But that man's father is my father's son."
What relation was the subject of the portrait to the speaker?

The Mysterious Obstacle

Undertake to clasp a person's hands in such manner that he cannot leave the room without unclasping them.
   How is it to be done?

The Bewitched Right Hand

Undertake to put something into a person's left hand which he cannot possibly take in his right.
   How is it to be done?

An Arithmetical Enigma

From a number that's odd cut off its head,
  It then will even be;
Its tail, I pray, next take away,
  Your mother then you'll see.

The Fasting Man

How many hard-boiled eggs can a hungry man eat on an empty stomach?

A Very Singular Subtraction

From six take nine, from nine take ten, from forty take fifty, and yet have six left.
  How is it to be done?

The Egg and the Cannonball

Exhibiting an egg and a cannonball, hold forth learnedly on the extraordinary strength of a perfect arch, and, still more, of a perfect dome, remarking that few people know how strong even the shell of an egg is, if it is placed in a proper position. In proof of your assertion, undertake to place the egg, without covering it in any way, in such a position that no one present can break it with the cannonball.

How is it to be done?

4

"Dissected" or Combination Puzzles

The number of these is legion. We all remember the "dissected maps" of our early youth, whereby we learnt geography (and very thoroughly, as far as it went), while we fondly imagined we were only amusing ourselves. With these, however, we have for our present purpose nothing to do. The present chapter will be primarily devoted to the large class of puzzles in which a given geometric figure is cut into pieces that must be rearranged into other figures and shapes.

The Extended Square

Required, to cut a cardboard square, as shown in the diagram below, into two pieces, so that by successive shiftings the pieces will form the parallelogram and the eccentric figure, also shown below.

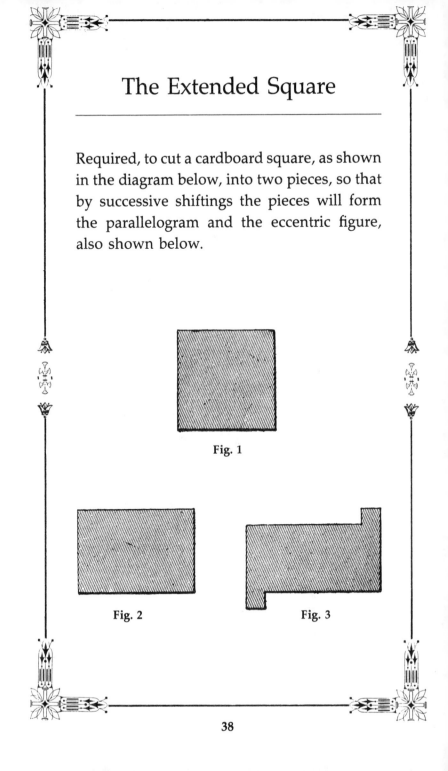

Fig. 1

Fig. 2   Fig. 3

The Two Squares

Given, a piece of paper or cardboard of the shape depicted below, a small square in juxtaposition with one four times its size.

Required, by two cuts (each in a straight line), to divide the piece of cardboard so that the resulting segments shall, differently arranged, form one perfect square.

The "Anchor" Puzzle

This consists of a square piece of cardboard divided into seven segments (two large triangles, *a*, *a*; a smaller one, *b*; and two still smaller, *c*, *c*; a square, *d*; and a rhomboid, *e*), as shown below. In Fig. 1 these pieces are arranged into a square. Even the rearrangement of these pieces back into a square, when once fairly mixed, will be found a matter of some little difficulty, but this is the smallest of the problems presented by the puzzle. Following are some of the different designs that may be formed by combining these pieces in different ways. All seven pieces must be used to form each design. It is a curious fact that some of those designs that are simplest in appearance are the most difficult to work out. No more aggravating, and at the same time fascinating, puzzles have come under our notice than this series.

Fig. 1

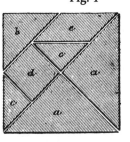

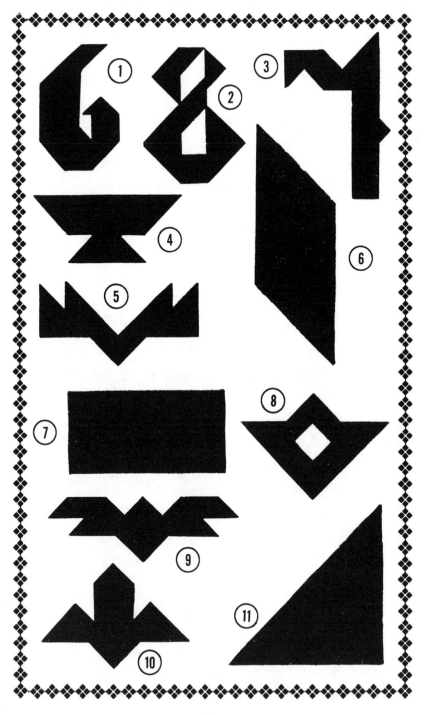

The Latin Cross Puzzle

Given, five pieces of paper or cardboard, one as *a*, one as *b*, and three as *c*, as shown in Fig. 1. Required, to form a Latin cross, as shown in Fig. 2, with these five pieces.

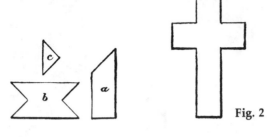

Fig. 1   Fig. 2

The Greek Cross Puzzle

Given, a piece of paper or cardboard in the form of a Greek or equal-armed cross, as shown below.

Required, by two straight cuts, to divide it so the pieces when reunited form a square.

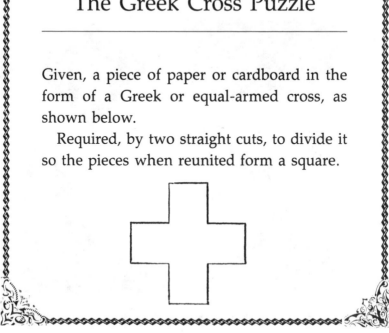

Eight Squares in One

Cut out eight squares of cardboard of equal size, and divide four of them diagonally from corner to corner. This will give you twelve pieces, four square and eight triangular.

Required, to arrange them to form a single perfect square.

The Carpenter's Puzzle

Given, a slip of wood, fifteen inches long by three inches wide.

How is it possible to cut it so that the pieces when rearranged form a perfect square?

The Five Squares

Given, five squares of cardboard, alike in size.

Required, to cut them, so that by rearrangement of the pieces you can form one large square.

The Cross-Keys or Three-Piece Puzzle

This is a very ingenious puzzle. It is one of the simplest, in one sense, being composed of only three pieces of wood, but they are interlocked with extreme ingenuity, and the endeavor to separate them will give a good deal of trouble. Indeed, one's first impression, on casual inspection, is that the whole must have been carved of a single piece.

Contrary to the usual rule, the reconstruction of the puzzle will here be found easier than its separation.

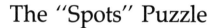

The "Spots" Puzzle

This puzzle is very much more difficult than it looks. It consists of a wooden cube, not quite three inches each way, cut into nine bars of equal size. Each of these is decorated with one or more spots half an inch in diameter.

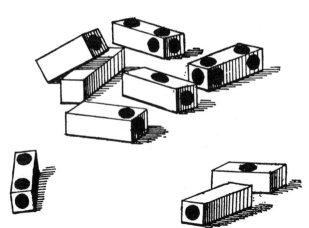

The experimenter is required to put together these bars in such manner that the resulting cube shall represent an enlarged model of the die familiar to the backgammon player (see below), with all its spots in proper position. These, it may be mentioned for the benefit of the uninitiated, are arranged as follows:—The ace point is opposite the six; the two opposite the five; and the three opposite the four; the total of each pair of opposite sides is always seven. A die that does not answer these conditions is regarded as fraudulent.

The Man of Many Parts

This is a puzzle of German origin. It consists of four cards, each about four inches in length by two in width, bearing respectively the designs shown below, being of men carrying their heads and limbs in various abnormal positions.

The experimenter is required to arrange the four cards to produce a single perfect figure.

The Diabolical Cube

This is a puzzle of a simple character, but one that will, nevertheless, give some trouble to anyone attempting it for the first time. It consists of six pieces, *a–f*, respectively, shaped as shown here.

Of these six segments the experimenter is required to form a cube. (Editor's note: The six pieces can easily be constructed using twenty-seven dice and glue.)

The Caricature Puzzle

This puzzle consists of the seven pieces that were used in the first puzzle in this chapter, the "Anchor."

With these, construct the grotesque representations of the human figure shown here. Space only allows half a dozen examples but the possible number of such combinations is extraordinary, and many of them are most comical in effect. See if you can faithfully construct each of the following figures.

5

Word and Letter Puzzles

A Puzzling Inscription

The following queer inscription is said to be found in the chancel of a small church in Wales, just over the Ten Commandments. The addition of a single letter, repeated at various intervals, renders it not only intelligible, but appropriate to the situation:

P R S V R Y P R F C T M N
V R K P T H S P R C P T S T N

What is the missing letter?

Scattered Sentiment

The following, duly rearranged, will be found to form a couplet suitable for a valentine.

Daruno em hslal verho,
Ni dasesns ro lege,
Lilt flie's rdaems eb vero,
Twees riemem's fo ethe.

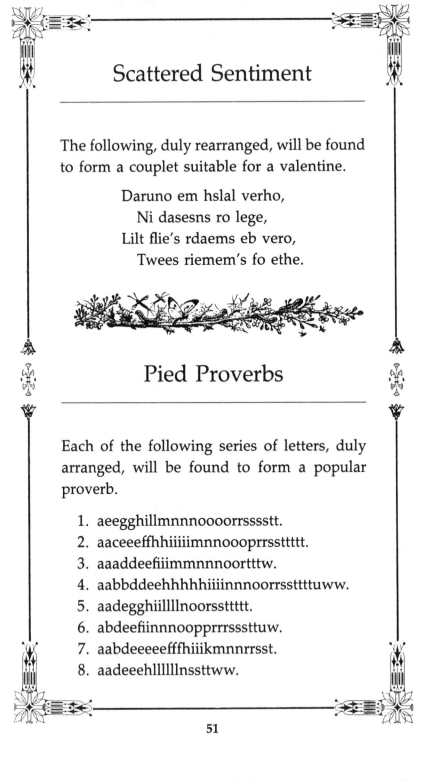

Pied Proverbs

Each of the following series of letters, duly arranged, will be found to form a popular proverb.

1. aeegghillmnnnoooorrssssstt.
2. aaceeeffhhiiiiimnnooopprrssttttt.
3. aaaddeefiiimmnnnnoortttw.
4. aabbddeehhhhhiiiinnnoorrssttttuww.
5. aadegghiillllnoorssttttt.
6. abdeefiinnnoopprrrssssttuw.
7. aabdeeeeefffhiiikmnnnrrsst.
8. aadeeehllllllnssttww.

An Easy One

Make one word of the following letters.

E D O R N O W

Dropped-Letter Proverbs

Supply the missing letters, and each of the series following will be found to represent a popular proverb. Each dash represents either a dropped letter or the space between two words. In some of the later examples one dash stands for two dropped letters.

1. A-t-t-h-n-t-m-s-v-s-n-n-.
2. F-i-t-h-a-t-e-e-w-n-a-r-a-y.
3. S-r-k-w-i-e-h-i-o-s-h-t.
4. H-l-g-s-b-s-w-o-a-g-s-l-t.
5. B-r-s-f-f-t-r-f-c-t-g-t-r.
6. H-w-o-g-s-b-r-w-g-g-s-s-r-w-g.
7. C-l-r-n-d-f-o-s-p-k-h-t-u-h.
8. W-e-t-e-w-n-s-n-h-w-t-s-t.
9. S-r-r-k-n-n-s-m-k-l-n-f-n-s.
10. H-n-s-y-s-t-b-s-p-l-c-.
11. T-k-c-r-f-h-p-n-n-t-e-p-n-s-w-l-t-k-c-r-f-t-e-s-l-s.

Dropped-Letter Nursery Rhymes

The following, the missing letters being duly supplied, will be found to represent familiar quotations of the juvenile order:

1. H-w-o-h-h-l-t-l-b-s-b-e
     I-p-o-e-a-h-h-n-n-h-u-;
     H-g-t-e-s-o-e-a-l-h-d-y
     F-o-e-e-y-p-n-n-f-o-e-.

2. J-c-a-d-i-l-e-t-p-h-h-l-
     T-f-t-h-p-i-o-w-t-r:
     J-c-f-l-d-w-a-d-r-k-h-s-r-w-
     A-d-i-l-a-e-u-b-i-g-f-e-.

3. H-y-i-d-e-i-d-e-h-c-t-n-t-e-i-d-l-
     T-e-o-j-m-e-o-e-t-e-o-n
     T-e-i-t-e-o-l-u-h-d-o-e-s-c-f-n-s-o-t
     A-d-h-d-s-r-n-w-y-i-h-h-s-o-n.

Transformations

This is a form of word puzzle that deserves to be better known, as it may be made productive of considerable amusement. It consists of taking a word and trying to see in how many moves, or transpositions, altering only one letter each time, it takes for you to transform it into another prearranged word of the same number of letters, but of different or opposite meaning; for example: light into heavy, rose into lily, hard into easy. Each step of the process must be a real word. Using the last pair as an example, five moves will suffice.

Hard—(1) card, (2) cart, (3) cast, (4) east, (5) Easy.

This, however, is a more than usually favorable specimen, one of the letters, *a*, being common to both words, and requiring no change. A considerably larger number of moves will usually be found necessary. Unless one or more letters are common to both words, the number of moves cannot possibly be *less* than the number of letters in each word.

Where several persons take part, this may be made a very amusing game. Certain pairs of words having been agreed upon, each takes the list and tries in how few moves he can effect the required transformations. The player with the smallest total wins the game.

The reader is invited to transform the following examples.

Hand into foot—in six moves.
Sin into woe—in three moves.
Hate into love—in three moves.
Black into white—in eight moves.
Wood into coal—in three moves.
Cat into dog—in three moves.
More into less—in four moves.
Rose into lily—in five moves.
Shoe into boot—in three moves.

Anagrams

An anagram is defined by Ogilvie as "the transposition of the letters of a name, by which a new word is formed." This definition hardly goes far enough, inasmuch as it ignores the far more interesting class of anagrams in which the letters of a whole sentence are rearranged to assume a different sense. To be worthy of serious consideration, however, the anagram must have a further quality—the new rendering must have some relation to the original. In some cases a new rendering of this kind has happened to be singularly appropriate; so much so, indeed, that in less enlightened times people have claimed for anagrams a sort of inspiration, or magical significance. There is a historic instance in the case of James I of England, whose name, *James Stuart*, was transposed by his courtiers, to his great delight, into *A just master*, and who was more than half persuaded of his descent from the mythical King Arthur, on the ground that his full name, *Charles James Stuart*, was capable of transposition into *Claims Arthur's Seat*. (Editor's note: It is necessary to substitute an "i" for the "j" for this to work.)

Here is a brief selection to exercise your ingenuity upon.

1. *Rare mad frolic.* Transposed, represents—a political cry.
2. *Got a scant religion:*—the name of a prominent division of Nonconformists.
3. *Best in prayer:*—ditto, ditto.
4. *City life:*—happiness.
5. *Tournament:*—a description of tilting.
6. *Melodrama:*—what melodrama ought to be.
7. *Misanthrope:*—what he deserves.
8. *Old England:*—the same country poetically described.
9. *Telegraphs:*—what they are to commerce.
10. *Lawyers:*—a satirical description of themselves.
11. *Astronomers:*—ditto.
12. *Astronomers:*—their occupation gone.

Beheaded Words

When you behead a word you drop the first letter, which leaves you with another word. Try your hand at the following nine "beheadings":—

1. Behead a tree, and leave the roof of a vault.
2. Behead "on high," and leave the topmost floor.
3. Behead "thrown violently," and leave an organ of the body.
4. Behead a preposition, and leave a contest.
5. Behead your own property, and leave ours.
6. Behead to delete, and leave to destroy.
7. Behead a reproach, and leave a relative.
8. Behead to annoy, and leave comfort.
9. Behead an occurrence, and leave an airhole.

The deleted initials, taken in the above order, will give the name of an American general, after whom a well-known street in Paris is named.

6

Miscellaneous Puzzles

To Balance an Egg on the Point of a Walking Stick

The articles to be employed in this puzzle are an egg, a cork, a gentleman's walking stick, and a couple of dinner forks.

Required, to balance the egg, by the aid of the other three articles, on the smaller end of the walking stick.

Crossette

Arrange in the form of a circle ten smaller circles (say, coins or counters), as shown below.

Starting from any circle you please, and calling such circle 1, and next 2, and so on, strike out the fourth. Then start again from any circle you please, count 1, 2, 3, 4, and strike out the fourth. Proceed as above until all but one have been struck out.

You may count either backwards or forwards. Circles already struck out are to be reckoned in counting, but the count of "four" must in each case fall upon a circle not already struck out.

This puzzle may be most conveniently worked with the aid of "reversi" counters, which, as the reader is probably aware, are red on the one side and black on the other. Ten of these are arranged in a circle, with the *red* side uppermost, and as each is "struck out" it is turned over, to bring the *black* side uppermost.

Skihi

This next item is sold as a game, but comes more properly within the category of puzzles. It is a patent, and the property of the Skihi Novelty Company, London, W.C.

The set consists of 48 square cards, 2 inches each way, and of various colors. Each card has four slots cut in it, as shown in Fig. 1. There are also 10 circular cards, each with three slots, as shown in Fig. 2.

These cards may be utilized to form an almost unlimited number of fanciful designs. We include a few examples, which will give some idea of the very wide capabilities of this clever toy. All of these may be constructed with a single set. By using three or four sets in conjunction, very much more ambitious designs may be executed.

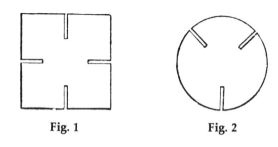

Fig. 1   Fig. 2

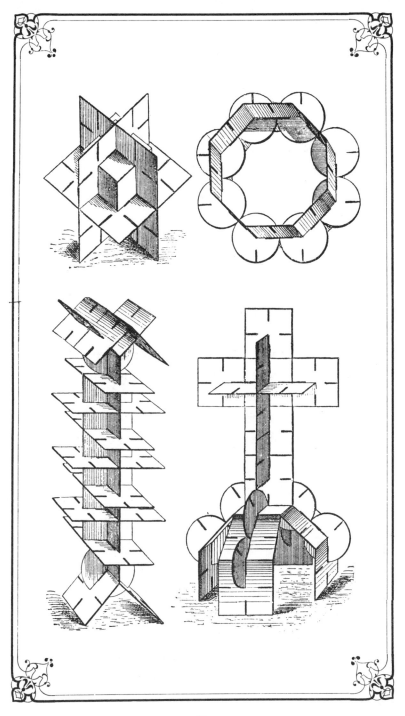

A Card Puzzle

Taking the four "fives" from a pack of cards, you are required to arrange them, face up-wards, in such manner that only four pips of each shall be visible.

Another Card Puzzle

Remove the aces and court cards from the pack. Arrange them in four rows in such manner that neither horizontally nor perpendicularly shall there be two of same rank or same suit in any one row.

The Cut Playing Card

Given, a playing card or an oblong piece of cardboard of the same size.

Required, to cut it, still keeping it in one piece, so a person of ordinary stature can pass through it.

The Four Wine Glasses

Given, four wine glasses of same shape and size.

Required, to arrange them so the center of the foot of any one is equidistant from all the rest.

The Balanced Coin

It would stagger most people to be invited to balance a coin on edge on the point of a needle, and yet, if you know how to do it, the feat is not only possible but easy.

The requirements for the trick are to be found in any household. They are a corked wine bottle, a second cork of somewhat smaller size, a needle, and a couple of dessert forks of equal size and weight. Last, but not least in importance, a coin. Two penknives, of equal size and weight, may be substituted for the forks.

Having provided himself with these items, the reader is invited to try whether he can solve the puzzle.

One Peg to Fit Three Holes

A brass plate has three openings, one circular, one square, and one triangular. The experimenter is handed a knife and a cork, which just passes through the circular hole. He is required to cut the cork so it fills any one of the three openings exactly.

A piece of stiff cardboard may be cut and substituted for the brass plate.

The Five Straws

Given, five straws, each three to four inches in length, and a coin.

Required, by holding the end of one straw only, to lift all the remainder.

The Two Dogs

The two dogs depicted below are obviously dead.

Required, by the addition of four more lines, to restore them to life again.

How is this done?

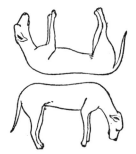

The Penetrative Coin

Cut a circular hole the size of an American nickel in a piece of stiff paper. Invite anyone to pass a quarter through the hole without touching the coin or tearing the paper. Most people will tell you this can't be done, because the diameter of a quarter is larger than the hole. And yet it *can* be done—easily done; and the reader is invited to find out how to do it.

The Fragmented Treasure

This puzzle comes from Germany, but is said to be of Oriental origin. The legend accompanying it is to the effect that an Eastern prince, Haroun al Elim, in far back times, ruled over a range of country with eight sugarloaf hills, on each of which was erected a fortress. Each fortress, with the surrounding district, was under the command of a governor, but the jealousies of the eight governors and their respective underlings led to fighting and bloodshed whenever they chanced to meet. To lessen the chance of such meetings, Haroun made a number of roads, eight crossing his kingdom in one direction, eight more at right angles to them, and others crossing diagonally. These were so arranged with reference to the castles that the occupants of each castle had a clear road in each direction through and out of the prince's territory without passing any other castle.

The castles, says the legend, are now in ruins, and the roads no longer traceable; but a plan of them is still preserved among the archives of the Mosque Al Redin, on the coast of the Red Sea. Unfortunately, the plan, which was folded in four, has been worn by age into four separate fragments, and the utmost skill of the qadi of the mosque has failed to discover their proper relative positions. He has therefore offered a reward—a treasure of ancient jewellery preserved at the mosque— to anyone who may succeed in placing the four fragments in their original positions— with no two castles on either road, either horizontal, perpendicular, or diagonal.

The severed map has been reproduced on the four separate cards pictured below, as *A*, *B*, *C*, and *D*.

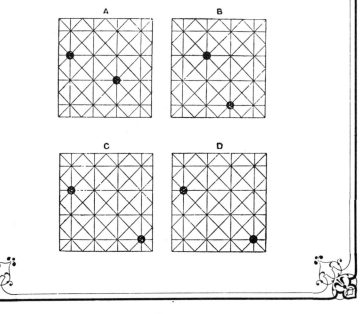

The Two Corks

Take two wine-bottle corks and hold each transversely across the fork of the thumb as shown in Fig. 1. Now with the thumb and second finger of the *right* hand take hold of the cork (placing one finger on each end) in the *left* hand, and, at the same time, with the thumb and second finger of the *left* hand take hold of the cork in the *right* hand, and draw them apart.

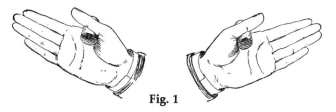

Fig. 1

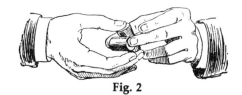

Fig. 2

The above sounds simple enough, but the neophyte will find that the corks are brought crosswise, as shown in Fig. 2. The puzzle is to avoid this and enable them to part freely.

The Balanced Pencil

Given, a lead pencil and a penknife, with which you sharpen the pencil to the finest possible point.

Required, to balance the pencil in an upright, or nearly upright, position on the tip of the forefinger.

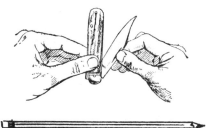

The Knotted Handkerchief

Required, to take a handkerchief, twisted ropewise, by its opposite ends and, *without letting go of either end*, to tie a knot in the middle.

7

Arithmetical Puzzles

The "Forty-Five" Puzzle

The number 45 has some curious properties. Among others, it may be divided into four parts, in such manner that if you add two to the first, subtract two from the second, multiply the third by two, and divide the fourth by two, in each case the result will be equal.

What are they?

The "Twenty-Six" Puzzle

This is a magic square with a difference, the four corner places being omitted. The problem is to arrange the numbers 1 to 12 in the form of a cross, as shown below, to make 26 in seven different ways—the two horizontal and the two vertical rows, the group of squares marked *a a a a*, the group marked *b b b b*, and the group marked *c c c c*, each making the above-mentioned total.

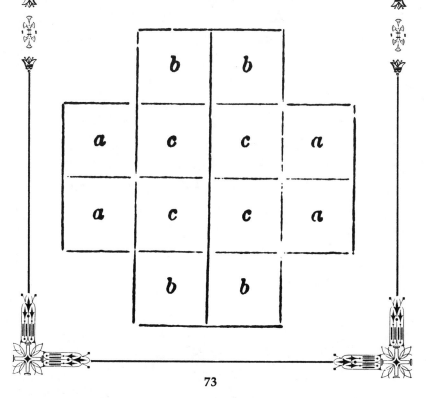

A Singular Subtraction

Required, to subtract 45 from 45 in such manner that there shall be 45 left.

An Unmanageable Legacy

An old farmer left a will bequeathing his horses to his three sons, John, James, and William, in the following proportions: John, the eldest, was to have one half, James, one-third, and William, one-ninth. When he died, however, the number of horses in his stable was seventeen, a number divisible neither by two, three, or nine. Perplexed, the three brothers consulted a lawyer, who hit on a clever scheme whereby the intentions of the old farmer were carried out to the satisfaction of all parties.

How was it managed?

A Novel Century

Required, by multiplication and addition of the numbers 1 to 9, to make 100, each number being used only once.

Another Century

Required, by addition only of the numbers 1 to 9 to make 100, each number being used once.

The Three Legacies

A gentleman making his will left legacies to his three servants. The parlormaid had been with him three times as long as the housemaid, and the cook twice as long as the parlormaid. He distributed his gifts in proportion to the length of service; and the total amount given was £70.

What was the amount received by each?

The Magic Cards

These are usually presented as a conjuring trick, but they also form a very effective puzzle, for it is clear that the secret must lie in the cards themselves, and, given sufficient acuteness, must be discoverable.

Prepare seven cards with numbers on them as shown here. (Editor's note: Duplicate and enlarge the cards with an office copier. Paste the copies on cardboard and cut the cards out.)

Request a person to think of any number from 1 to 127 and to state on which one or

I.			
1	33	65	97
3	35	67	99
5	37	69	101
7	39	71	103
9	41	73	105
11	43	75	107
13	45	77	109
15	47	79	111
17	49	81	113
19	51	83	115
21	53	85	117
23	55	87	119
25	57	89	121
27	59	91	123
29	61	93	125
31	63	95	127

II.			
2	34	66	98
3	35	67	99
6	38	70	102
7	39	71	103
10	42	74	106
11	43	75	107
14	46	78	110
15	47	79	111
18	50	82	114
19	51	83	115
22	54	86	118
23	55	87	119
26	58	90	122
27	59	91	123
30	62	94	126
31	63	95	127

III.			
4	36	68	100
5	37	69	101
6	38	70	102
7	39	71	103
12	44	76	108
13	45	77	109
14	46	78	110
15	47	79	111
20	52	84	116
21	53	85	117
22	54	86	118
23	55	87	119
28	60	92	124
29	61	93	125
30	62	94	126
31	63	95	127

more of the seven cards it is to be found. Anyone knowing the secret can instantly name the chosen number.

How is the number ascertained?

IV.			
8	40	72	104
9	41	73	105
10	42	74	106
11	43	75	107
12	44	76	108
13	45	77	109
14	46	78	110
15	47	79	111
24	56	88	120
25	57	89	121
26	58	90	122
27	59	91	123
28	60	92	124
29	61	93	125
30	62	94	126
31	63	95	127

V.			
16	48	80	112
17	49	81	113
18	50	82	114
19	51	83	115
20	52	84	116
21	53	85	117
22	54	86	118
23	55	87	119
24	56	88	120
25	57	89	121
26	58	90	122
27	59	91	123
28	60	92	124
29	61	93	125
30	62	94	126
31	63	95	127

VI.			
32	48	96	112
33	49	97	113
34	50	98	114
35	51	99	115
36	52	100	116
37	53	101	117
38	54	102	118
39	55	103	119
40	56	104	120
41	57	105	121
42	58	106	122
43	59	107	123
44	60	108	124
45	61	109	125
46	62	110	126
47	63	111	127

VII.			
64	80	96	112
65	81	97	113
66	82	98	114
67	83	99	115
68	84	100	116
69	85	101	117
70	86	102	118
71	87	103	119
72	88	104	120
73	89	105	121
74	90	106	122
75	91	107	123
76	92	108	124
77	93	109	125
78	94	110	126
79	95	111	127

The Captives in the Tower

An elderly queen, her daughter, and son, weighing 195 pounds, 105 pounds, and 90 pounds, respectively, were kept prisoners at the top of a high tower. The only communication with the ground was a cord passing over a pulley with a basket at each end. It was arranged so that when one basket rested on the ground the other was opposite the window. Naturally, if the one were more heavily loaded than the other, the heavier would descend; but if the excess on either side was more than 15 pounds, the descent became dangerously rapid, and from the position of the rope the captives could not stop it with their hands. The only thing available to help them in the tower was a cannonball weighing 75 pounds. They, notwithstanding, contrived to escape.

How did they manage it?

The Two Travellers

A and B are travelling the same road, A going four miles an hour, B going five miles an hour. But A has a two-and-a-half-hour lead.

In what length of time will B overtake A, and how far from the starting point?

The Wolf, the Goat, and the Cabbages

A boatman has to ferry across a stream a wolf, a goat, and a basket of cabbages. His boat is so small that only one of the three, besides himself, can be contained in it. How is he to manage, so that the wolf shall have no opportunity of killing the goat, or the goat of eating up the cabbages?

Can You Name It?

Required, to find a number which is just so much short of 50 as its quadruple is above 50.

A Curious Number

A certain number is divisible into four parts in such manner that the first part is 500 times, the second 400 times, and the third 40 times as much as the last and smallest part.

What is the number, and what are the several parts?

Eleven Guests in Ten Beds

An innkeeper had a sudden influx of guests, eleven arriving in one party, and demanding beds. The host had only ten beds at his disposal, but he managed to accommodate them as follows: He put two in the first bed, with the understanding that the second should have a bed to himself after a brief interval; he then put the third in the second bed, the fourth in the third bed, and so on, the tenth being accommodated in the ninth bed. He had thus one bed still left, which the eleventh man, now sleeping double in the first bed, was invited to occupy.

It is clear that there must be a fallacy somewhere, but where does it lie?

ANSWERS

"New Oxford Street, home of Bland's Magical Palace! All out for them that needs to be checking their answers to the problems in "Great Victorian Puzzle Book." You'll be finding Professor Hoffmann inside with the solutions to all your problems! Step lively now, I ain't got all day, you know!"

And now for the answers! Professor Hoffmann has done his best to make the solutions as clear as possible. Occasionally, a puzzle will have more than one solution. When this happens, the professor gives you the answer that is most often associated with the problem. Sometimes a puzzle will have so many solutions that it is not practical to give more than one. Thankfully, most problems in this book have only one solution.

Problem Using Eleven Counters (page 10). The eleven counters are arranged as shown here. The five at bottom count as two rows of three, the counter in the middle being common to both.

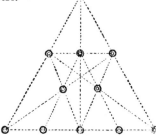

Problem Using Nine Counters (page 10). Arrange the nine counters as shown here.

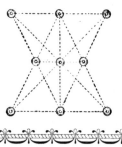

Problem Using Twenty-Seven Counters (page 10).

There are several different arrangements that will answer the conditions of this problem. Pictured below are two such arrangements.

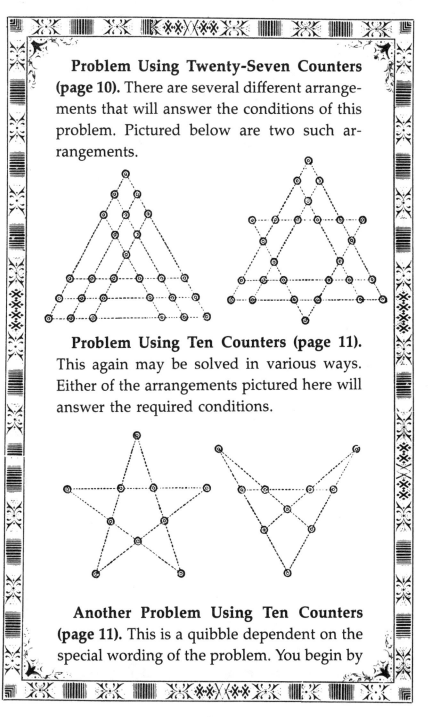

Problem Using Ten Counters (page 11).

This again may be solved in various ways. Either of the arrangements pictured here will answer the required conditions.

Another Problem Using Ten Counters (page 11).

This is a quibble dependent on the special wording of the problem. You begin by distributing the counters in three rows of three each, forming a square, and then place the remaining counter on the middle one. You have now four rows of four each; but as each row can be counted in two different directions, from right to left or left to right, and vertical rows upwards or downwards, you are enabled to count four in eight different directions, as required by the problem.

Problem Using Nineteen Counters (page 11). The nineteen counters should be arranged as shown below.

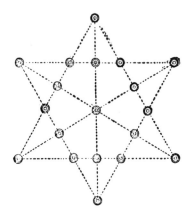

The Monastery Problem (page 12). The secret lies in increasing or diminishing, as the case may require, the number of persons in the corner cells, each of which counts twice over, and so, to a person as doddering as the abbot must be assumed to have been, seems at first sight to increase the general total. Thus when the four monks absented themselves, the remaining twenty were rearranged as in Fig. 1; and when they returned with four other persons, the twenty-eight were disposed as in Fig. 2. When four more visitors arrived, the thirty-two were distributed as in Fig. 3; and when the final four arrived, the party, now numbering thirty-six, were arranged as in Fig. 4.

Fig. 1   Fig. 2   Fig. 3   Fig. 4

The Eight-Pointed Star Problem (page 14). The secret lies in working backwards throughout, each time covering the point from which you last started. Thus, placing a counter on *a*, draw it along the line *a d*, and leave it on *d*. *a* is now the next point to be covered, and there is only one vacant line, *f a*, which leads to it. Place, therefore, your second counter on *f*, draw it along *f a*, and leave it on *a*. The third counter must be placed on *c*, drawn along *c f*, and left on *f*. The next is placed on *h*, and left on *c*. The fifth is placed on *e*, and left on *h*. The sixth is placed on *b*, and left on *e*; and the seventh is placed on *g*, and left on *b*.

You now have the whole seven counters duly placed, and only one point, *g*, left uncovered.

The "Crowning" Puzzle (page 15). Imagine the row of counters is indicated by the following numbers: 1, 2, 3, 4, 5, 6, 7, 8, 9, 10. Proceed as follows: Place 4 on 1, 6 on 9, 8 on 3, 2 on 5, and 10 on 7. Or place 4 on 1, 7 on 3, 5 on 9, 2 on 6, and 10 on 8.

There are several formulas which will answer the problem, but a person trying the puzzle for the first time will find some difficulty in hitting upon one of them.

An Intersection Problem (page 16). The counters must be placed as shown below.

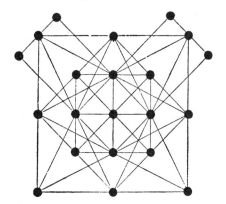

The "Right and Left" Puzzle (page 17). The key to this puzzle lies in the observance of the following rules:

1. After having moved a counter, one *of the opposite color* must invariably be passed over it.

2. After having passed one counter over another, the next advance will be *with the*

same color as such first-mentioned counter. The position will guide you whether to move or to pass over, only one of such alternatives usually being open to you.

The above rules, however, only apply up to a certain point. After the ninth move you will find that the next should be with a counter of the same color; but none such is available. By this time, however, the puzzle is practically solved. The counters are white and red alternately, with the space to the extreme left vacant, and two or three obvious moves place the counters so as to answer the conditions of the problem.

Thus, if we begin with the white counters, the moves will be as below (see Fig. 1), the

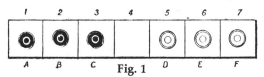

Fig. 1

spaces being designated by the numbers, and counters by the letters:

1. D moves into space 4
2. C passes over D into space 5
3. B moves into space 3
4. D passes over B into space 2
5. E passes over C into space 4
6. F moves into space 6
7. C passes over F into space 7
8. B passes over E into space 5
9. A passes over D into space 3

Here occurs the state of things to which we have referred: the position being as in Fig. 2.

The next move should, according to the

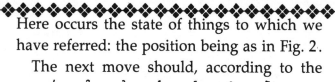

Fig. 2

rule, be with a red counter; but there is only one counter, and that a white one, D, which is capable of being moved in a forward direction, and that *only* into 1. This move is made accordingly, and the solution proceeds as follows, the remaining moves being almost a matter of course:

10. D moves into space 1
11. E passes over A into space 2
12. F passes over B into space 4
13. B moves into space 6
14. A passes over F into space 5
15. F moves into space 3, and the trick is done.

If the operator prefers to begin with the *red* counters, the moves will be as follows:

1. C moves into 4
2. D passes over into 3
3. E move into 5
4. C passes over into 6
5. B passes over into 4
6. A moves into 2
7. D passes over into 1
8. E passes over into 3
9. F passes over into 5

(From this point, as before, the rule ceases to apply.)

10. C moves into 7
11. B passes over into 6
12. A passes over into 4
13. E moves into 2
14. F passes over into 3
15. A moves into 5

When the principle is mastered, the movements can be executed with great rapidity and with little fear of any onlooker being able to repeat them from recollection.

The solution we have given is equally applicable to any larger (even) number of counters, so long as the number of spaces be one greater, and a vacant space be left in the middle.

Another "Right and Left" Puzzle (page 18). You first deal with the middle row (15 to 21) after the manner described in the last solution. You then move the white counter now occupying space 25 into the central space (18), and deal in like manner with the fourth row (22 to 28), leaving space 25 vacant. Pass the counter occupying 11 into this space, and you are then in a position to deal with the second row (8 to 14). When space 11 is again vacant, move the counter occupying space 4 into it, and you are then enabled to deal with the uppermost line (1 to 7).

Pass the counter occupying space 18 into space 4, and that occupying space 32 into space 18. You are now in a position to rearrange the last row (29 to 35). You have then a vacant space (32) in the middle of the bottom row. Move the counter occupying space 25 into this space, then pass that occupying 11 into 25, and finally move the counter now in 18 into 11.

The "Four and Four" Puzzle (page 19). The necessary transpositions are as follows:

Shift the counters occupying spaces 2 and 3 to 9 and 10; shift the counters occupying spaces 5 and 6 to 2 and 3; shift the counters occupying spaces 8 and 9 to 5 and 6; shift the counters occupying spaces 1 and 2 to 8 and 9.

To work the counters back again, you have merely to reverse the process, but to do this from memory is rather more difficult than the original puzzle, and some amount of practice is necessary before it can be done with facility.

The "English Sixteen" Puzzle (page 20). We know of no rule for working this puzzle. There are several possible solutions. Among others, moving the men in the following order will be found to answer the conditions of the problem. The man to be moved is in each case indicated by the number of the square in the puzzle drawing. It is not necessary to specify the square to which he is to be moved. As there is never more than one square vacant, the experimenter cannot well go wrong in this particular.

It will be observed that the number of moves is 52, which we believe to be the smallest that will suffice to transfer the whole of the men.

11, 7, 9, 8, 10, 13, 11, 14, 9, 6, 8, 5, 7, 11, 9, 10, 8, 2, 1, 6, 3, 5, 7, 4, 9, 12, 15, 17, 14, 16, 13, 15, 11, 7, 9, 14, 11, 13, 10, 8, 9, 6, 8, 2, 5, 7, 11, 9, 12, 10, 8, 9.

Problem Using Eleven Matches (page 22). Place the matches to form the word **NINE**.

Problem Using Nine Matches (page 23). Place the matches to form the number **XXXVI,** the Roman equivalent for 36.

A Triangle Puzzle (page 23). Place three of the matches on the table in the form of a triangle, and hold the remaining three above them so as to form a triangular pyramid, as shown below, *a b c* representing the base, and *d* the apex.

A Bridge of Matches (page 23). The three matches are interlaced as below, one resting on the brim of each wine glass. The weight binds them together, so that they will sustain a fourth wine glass without difficulty. Tobacco pipes (long clays) are sometimes used instead of matches and made to support a tankard, with even better effect.

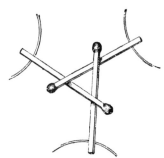

A Match Square Problem (page 24). Take away the matches forming the inner sides of the four corner squares, when you will have left two squares only, the one inside the other, as shown here.

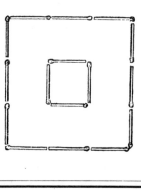

The Seventeen Match Puzzle (page 24).
Take away the two matches forming each of
the upper corners, and the middle match of
the lower side. This will leave three squares
only, as shown below.

**Another Seventeen Match Puzzle (page
25).** Take away the four matches forming the
inner sides of the four squares to the left, and
the two matches forming the outer sides of
the lower square to the right. You will then
have only two squares left, a larger and a
smaller, as shown in the illustration.

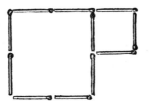

The Fifteen Matches Puzzle (page 25).
Victory will always lie with the player who
removes the tenth match, leaving five on the
table. Thus suppose **A** and **B** to be the players,
and **B** to have the move, five matches being
left. If **B** now removes 1, **A** removes 3; if **B**
removes 2, **A** removes 2; if **B** removes 3, **A**
removes 1; in each case leaving the last to be
removed by **B**.

After one or two trials, the novice will probably perceive that five is the critical remainder, and will endeavor to leave that number. To prevent his doing so, his adversary must so play in the earlier stages of the game as to leave *nine* matches, when it will be equally impossible for the novice to leave five for, again, if **B** plays 1, **A** will play 3; if **B** plays 2, **A** will play 2; if **B** plays 3, **A** will play 1; and five will be left, with **B** to play.

In like manner, to make sure of leaving *nine*, the adept plays in the first instance so as to leave thirteen, *i.e.*, if he is the first to play, he removes *two*.

Between two players both of whom know the secret, the first must necessarily win.

A Match-Shifting Problem (page 26). Take away the two matches forming the outer sides of the upper right-hand square, and the two forming the outer sides of the lower left-hand square. You have then left two squares lying diagonally. With the four matches you have removed, form a third square in continuation of the diagonal line, and you will have three squares, as shown below.

Another Match-Shifting Problem (page 26). Remove the middle match of the upper side of the figure, and the two matches forming the outer sides of the lower square to the right, as shown here.

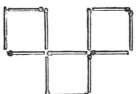

An Uplifting Puzzle (page 27). Take the fourth match in your hand, and with its point gently raise the two joined matches to a slightly more vertical position, so the upper end of the third match falls forward into the angle of the other two, as shown in the illustration below. By slightly raising the fourth match you lock all three together, and they may be lifted without difficulty.

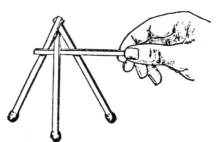

Subtraction Extraordinary (page 28). Write nineteen in Roman numerals: **XIX**. Remove the **I**, and you have **XX**.

A New Way of Writing 100 (page 29). The answer is: $99\frac{99}{99} = 100$.

A Queer Query (page 30). This is a mere "sell." The answer is "Letters." In the word "twenty" there are six letters, in the word "six" three, and so on.

Multiplication Extraordinary (page 31). The answer is: $1\frac{1}{5}$. $1\frac{1}{5} \times 5 = 6$.

Two Halves Greater Than the Whole (page 29). Write twelve in Roman numerals—**XII.** Halve the number by drawing a line horizontally through the middle, and the upper half is **VII.**

The Family Party (page 29). The party consisted of three children (two girls and a boy), their father and mother, and their father's father and mother. It will be found that these, in their various relations to each other, fill all the characters named. Thus the father, in relation to his own father, is also a son, and so on.

The Flying Coin (page 30). Place yourself so as to bring one hand just over the mantelpiece, and drop the coin contained in such hand upon the latter. Then, keeping the arms still extended, turn the body round till the other hand comes over the coin. Pick it up, and you have solved the puzzle, both coins being now in the one hand.

Three Times Six (page 30). The answer is: $6\frac{6}{6} = 7$.

The Last Thing Out (page 31). The puzzle is solved by cracking a nut, showing your interlocutor the kernel, and then eating it.

The Mysterious Addition (page 31). 1. Write five in roman characters (**V**); add **I**, and it becomes **IV**. 2. The Letter **S**, which makes **IX SIX**.

The Three Gingerbread Nuts (page 32). This is a very ancient "sell," but it still finds victims. The performer's undertaking is performed by simply putting on the hat selected. No one can deny that the three nuts are thereby brought under the hat.

Magic Made Easy (page 33). This puzzle depends on a double meaning. The spectators naturally prepare themselves for some more or less adroit feat of jugglery, but you perform your undertaking by simply crossing the closed hands. The right hand (and the coin in it) is now where the left was previously, and *vice versa.*

The Portrait (page 34). The portrait represented the speaker's son, as will be seen after a moment's consideration. The speaker says in effect, "The father of that man is my father's son"; in which case the father of the subject must be either a brother of the speaker, or himself. He has already told us that he has no brother. He himself must therefore be the father, and the portrait represents his son.

The Mysterious Obstacle (page 34). You perform your undertaking by clasping the person's hands round the leg of a large table, a piano, or other object too bulky to be dragged through the doorway.

The Bewitched Right Hand (page 34). You place in the person's left hand *his own right elbow*, which, obviously, he cannot take in his right hand.

An Arithmetical Enigma (page 35). The answer is: **SEVEN—EVEN—EVE.**

The Fasting Man (page 35). One only; for after eating one his stomach would no longer be empty.

A Very Singular Subtraction (page 35).

$$
\begin{array}{rrr}
\text{SIX} & \text{IX} & \text{XL} \\
-\ \text{IX} & \underline{\text{X}} & \underline{\text{L}} \\
\hline
\text{S} & \text{I} & \text{X}
\end{array}
$$

The Egg and the Cannonball (page 36). Place the egg on the floor in one corner of the room. The walls on either side then make it impossible to touch it with the cannonball.

The Extended Square (page 38). The card is cut as indicated in Fig. 1. The upper part is then shifted backwards one step, to form Fig. 2, or two steps, to form Fig. 3.

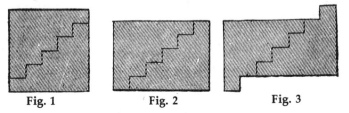

Fig. 1   Fig. 2   Fig. 3

The Two Squares (page 39). First divide the larger square by pencil lines from a to b, and c to d, then cut from e to c, and from c to f (see Fig. 1). The card will now be in three pieces, which, duly rearranged, will form a square, as shown in Fig. 2.

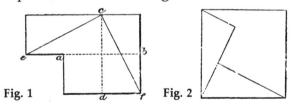

Fig. 1   Fig. 2

The "Anchor" Puzzle (page 40). The first step towards the solution of puzzles of this class is to study the relative proportions of the various segments, and note what results can be obtained from the combination of a given pair. These will, of course, vary according to the particular manner in which the two parts are brought into juxtaposition, and a slight alteration in this respect will often supply the solution of an apparently hopeless puzzle.

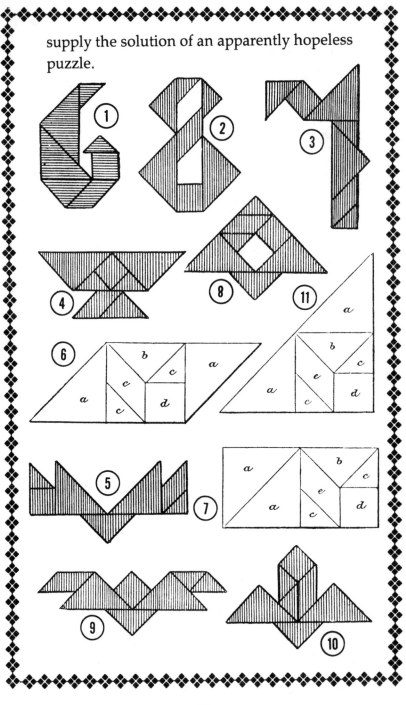

The Latin Cross Puzzle (page 42). The segments are arranged as shown below.

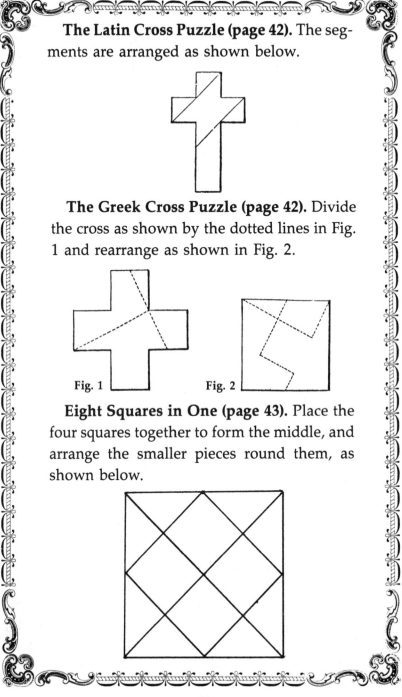

The Greek Cross Puzzle (page 42). Divide the cross as shown by the dotted lines in Fig. 1 and rearrange as shown in Fig. 2.

Fig. 1

Fig. 2

Eight Squares in One (page 43). Place the four squares together to form the middle, and arrange the smaller pieces round them, as shown below.

The Carpenter's Puzzle (page 43). The piece of wood is cut as indicated in Fig. 1, and pieces rearranged as shown in Fig. 2.

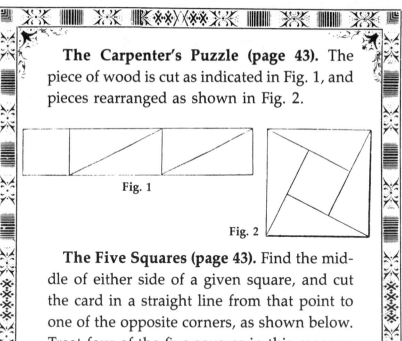

Fig. 1

Fig. 2

The Five Squares (page 43). Find the middle of either side of a given square, and cut the card in a straight line from that point to one of the opposite corners, as shown below. Treat four of the five squares in this manner. Rearrange the eight segments thus made with the uncut square in the middle, as shown below, and you will have a single perfect square.

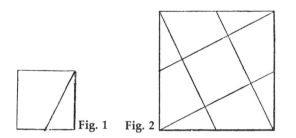

Fig. 1   Fig. 2

The Cross Keys or Three-Piece Puzzle (page 44). The three pieces of which the puzzle is composed are shaped as *a*, *b*, and *c*, respectively.

To put them together, take *a* upright between the forefinger and thumb of the left hand. Through the slot push *b*, with the cross-cut uppermost, till the farther edge of the central slot comes all but flush with the outer face of *a*. Then take *c*, with the short arm of the cross towards you, and lower it gently down over the top of *a*, the uncut middle portion (next to the short arm of the cross) passing through the cross-cut in *b*. You have now only to push *b* onward through *a* till the transverse cut is hidden, and the cross is complete.

To separate the parts, reverse the process.

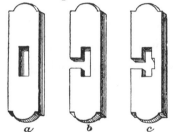

The "Spots" Puzzle (page 45). It will be found a great assistance towards the solution of this puzzle if you place a die on the table and work from it by way of model. We will assume, for the purpose of our explanation, that it is placed as shown below, the *six* being to the front, and, consequently, the *one* to the rear; the *two* at top, consequently the *five* at bottom; and the *four* to the *left*, consequently the *three* to the right, on the side concealed from view.

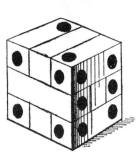

The lower stratum will consist of three bars as follows:

The hinder bar: Two spots on the under side, and one on the end to the left.

Middle: One spot in the middle of the under side. Otherwise blank.

Front: Two spots on the under side, two in the front, and one on each end.

We next come to the middle layer; and here most people give themselves a good deal of unnecessary trouble by taking it for granted that all the nine bars must lie *in the same direction.* As a matter of fact, the three at the top and three at the bottom should lie parallel, but the three in the middle are at right angles to them. This middle layer is thus formed as follows:

Left-hand: The bar with one spot on the end is towards the front. Otherwise blank.

Middle: The bar with one spot is on the hinder end. Otherwise blank.

Right-hand: The bar with a spot is on the

forward end, and one is in the middle of the right-hand side.

(These, as we have said, are to be laid *across* the three bars already placed.)

The upper layer is formed as follows:

Back: A spot on each end and one on the upper side to the right. The farther side is blank.

Middle: Blank throughout.

Front: Two spots on the front, one on the end to the left, and one on the top, at the same end.

These last three bars are laid on the top parallel to the bottom section, and the die is complete, with the appearance shown in the figure.

The Man of Many Parts (page 47). The secret lies in so arranging the cards that one half of each shall lap over half of the one next to it, thereby covering up its more eccentric features, and leaving visible only such half of the card as contributes to the desired result, which is as shown below.

The Diabolical Cube (page 48). Stand the piece *c* (the one that looks like a flight of steps) up on end, and beside it piece *a*, with its projecting portion uppermost, but farthest away from the highest step of *c*. Against the nearer side of *c* place the square block *e*, and stand the small block *f* on end beside it. The state of things will now be as shown in the drawing below. Fix *d* in beside *a*, with one of its projections pointing downwards and the other resting on *f*. You will find that you have now only room left for the remaining piece, *b*, whose cut-out central space just fits the projecting top of *c*. Place this in position, and the cube is complete.

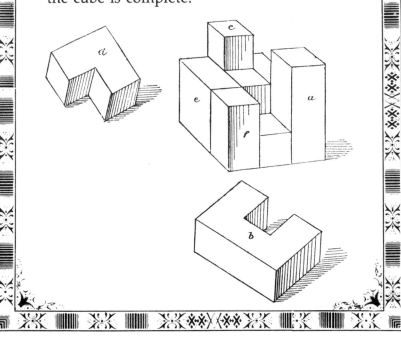

The Caricature Puzzle (page 49). The answers to the six figures are shown below. A host of other figures, equally comical, may be formed after a similar fashion.

A Puzzling Inscription (page 50). The letter **E**, which, inserted at the proper intervals, makes the inscription read:

PERSEVERE YE PERFECT MEN,
EVER KEEP THESE PRECEPTS TEN

Scattered Sentiment (page 51). The lines should read as follows:

Around me shall hover,
In sadness or glee,
Till life's dreams be over,
Sweet mem'ries of thee.

Pied Proverbs (page 51).
1. Rolling stones gather no moss.
2. Procrastination is the thief of time.
3. Time and tide wait for no man.
4. A bird in the hand is worth two in the bush.
5. All is not gold that glitters.
6. Fine words butter no parsnips.
7. Fine feathers make fine birds.
8. All's well that ends well.

An Easy One (page 52). This is a problem of the "quibble" order. The seven letters duly arranged form **one word.**

Dropped-Letter Proverbs (page 52).
1. A stitch in time saves nine.
2. Faint heart never won fair lady.
3. Strike while the iron's hot.
4. He laughs best who laughs last.
5. Birds of a feather flock together.
6. He who goes a-borrowing goes a-sorrowing.
7. Children and fools speak the truth.
8. When the wine is in, the wit is out.
9. Short reckonings make long friends.
10. Honesty is the best policy.
11. Take care of the pence, and the pounds will take care of themselves.

Dropped-Letter Nursery Rhymes (page 53).

1. How doth the little busy bee
   Improve each shining hour;
   He gathers honey all the day
   From every opening flower.

2. Jack and Jill went up the hill
   To fetch a pail of water;
   Jack fell down and broke his crown,
   And Jill came tumbling after.

3. Hey diddle diddle, the cat and the fiddle,
   The cow jumped over the moon,
   The little dog laughed to see such fine sport,
   And the dish ran away with the spoon.

Transformations (page 54).

Hand; hard; lard; lord; ford; fort*; foot.

Sin; son; won; woe.

Hate; have; lave; love.

Black; slack; stack; stalk; stale*; shale; whale; while; white.

Wood; wool; cool; coal.

Cat; cot; cog; dog.

More; lore; lose; loss; less.

Rose; lose; lost; list; lilt; lily.

Shoe; shot; soot; boot.

(*These are examples of a necessity, which frequently arises, of interposing a move which does not directly aid the transformation, but indirectly as a link with some more desirable word. In the first example, the word "food" might, in place of "fort," form the intermediate step between "ford" and "foot.")

Anagrams (page 56).

1. Radical reform
2. Congregationalist
3. Presbyterian
4. Felicity
5. To run at men
6. Made moral
7. Spare him not
8. Golden Land
9. Great helps
10. Sly ware
11. Moon-starers
12. No more stars

Beheaded Words (page 58).

1. L-arch
2. A-loft
3. F-lung
4. A-bout
5. Y-ours
6. E-rase
7. T-aunt
8. T-ease
9. E-vent

The initials give the name Lafayette.

To Balance an Egg on the Point of a Walking Stick (page 59). Have the egg boiled hard. It is said that the feat is possible even with a raw egg, but it is in this case much more difficult, the contents of the egg being in a condition of unstable equilibrium. Thrust the two forks into the cork, one on each side, so that they shall form an angle of about 60° to each other. Hold the stick, ferule upwards, firmly between the knees. Place the egg on end upon the ferule, and the cork on top of it, as shown below. After a few trials you will be able to balance the egg in an erect position.

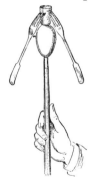

Crossette (page 60). It will be found that unless the experimenter proceeds in accordance with a regular system he will fail, the count of four beginning very soon to fall upon circles already crossed out.

To solve the puzzle, after striking out a given circle, *miss three before starting again.* Thus, suppose the start to be made from 1 to 4 will in such case be the first to be struck

1
10 2
9 3
8 4
7 5
6

out. Miss three, and start again at 8. Next, 1 will be struck out. Begin again at 5, and strike out 8. Again at 2, and strike out 5. Again at 9, and strike out 2. Again at 6, and strike out 9. Again at 3, and strike out 6. Again at 10, and strike out 3. Again at 7, and strike out 10.

You have thus struck out nine of the ten circles.

It will be observed that you strike out at each round the number with which you started at the previous round.

Skihi (page 62). For the formation of the Skihi designs nothing more is needed than a modicum of the constructive faculty, supplemented by a good stock of perseverance. The cards must be coaxed, not forced, into position. If this caution be borne in mind, and the diagram carefully studied beforehand, the execution of the most elaborate design becomes a mere matter of time and patience.

We will take, by way of example, the Maltese cube. Though so simple in appearance, it is by no means one of the easiest to construct, no less than eighteen cards being employed, and some little skill being needed to join them neatly together.

First take the card that is to form the top of the central or "solid" portion, and with this combine, by means of the slots, the four cards that are to form the uprights of the upper portion. Slot must be inserted into slot, and each card pushed well home. We next add the four cards which form the four sides of the cube (only the upper portions of which are visible in the diagram). These duly in place, we insert the four cards that form the horizontal platform in that middle; and this is a more difficult task, for each such card has to be worked into one of the angles of the cube. When these four are in position, the next thing to be done is to join together five cards as we did in the first instance (four round one middle card) and, when joined, unite these to the figure already made. Our cube is now complete; and by following the same method of construction it will be easy to put together either of the other figures. A little powdered French chalk rubbed into the slots will be found very useful to diminish friction. The cards when new are apt to go somewhat stiffly.

A Card Puzzle (page 64). The four cards are arranged as shown below, one pip of each being hidden by the overlapping corner of the next.

Another Card Puzzle (page 64). First take the four aces, and with them form one of the diagonal rows, beginning from the top left-hand corner. We will suppose that their order is ace of spades, ace of clubs, ace of hearts, ace of diamonds. Next take the kings, and with them form the second diagonal, bearing in mind that the two middle kings must be of the opposite suits to the two middle aces—in this case the king of spades and king of diamonds. Next place the four queens, beginning with the two squares next the top right-hand corner, and then filling the corresponding squares next the left-hand bottom corner. A very little consideration will show you

Ace of Spades	Knave of Hearts	Queen of Diamonds	King of Clubs
Knave of Diamonds	Ace of Clubs	King of Spades	Queen of Hearts
Queen of Clubs	King of Diamonds	Ace of Hearts	Knave of Spades
King of Hearts	Queen of Spades	Knave of Clubs	Ace of Diamonds

which queen should occupy each space. Then place the four knaves in the remaining spaces, duly bearing in mind the conditions, and you will finally have the arrangement shown in the drawing.

The arrangement will, of course, be subject to variation according to the cards with which you elect to commence.

The Cut Playing Card (page 64). Fold the card down the middle and cut through the line thus made to within a quarter of an inch of each end. See Fig. 1. Next, with a sharp penknife, cut through both thicknesses, alternately to right and left, but each time stopping within a quarter of an inch of the edge. See Fig. 2. The cuts should be about an eighth of an inch apart. The card when opened will resemble Fig. 3. Open it out still farther, when it will form an endless strip, of such a size as to pass easily over a person's body.

Fig. 1 Fig. 2 Fig. 3

The Four Wine Glasses (page 65). Place three of the wine glasses on the table so as to form an equilateral triangle, each side being equal to the height of a single glass. Then place the fourth glass upside down in the middle.

The Balanced Coin (page 65). The first step is to fix the needle, point upwards, in the cork of the wine bottle. The next is to cut a slit, a quarter of an inch deep, across the top of the smaller cork, and to press the coin as far as it will go into the cut so made. (The diagram is hardly accurate in this particular. The slit in the cork should be deep enough to admit about one half the diameter of the coin.) Holding the cork with the coin downwards, thrust the two forks into it (one on either side) in an upward direction, at an angle of about 30 degrees to the middle of the cork. Now bring the edge of the coin carefully down upon the point of the needle, as shown in the drawing, and if the forks are properly adjusted, it will remain balanced, and the cork may even be spun round at considerable speed with little fear of displacing it.

One Peg to Fit Three Holes (page 66). It will be observed that one side of the "square" is just equal in length to the diameter of the "circle." Cut the cork to the length shown in Fig. 1. If it is inserted sideways, it will then just fit the square hole. It already fits the cir-

Fig. 1 Fig. 2

cular hole. To adapt it to fit the triangular space also, draw a straight line across one end of it through the middle, and from such line cut an equal section in a sloping direction down to each side of the circular base. The cork will then assume the shape of Fig. 2 and will fit either one of the three holes.

The Five Straws (page 66). Interlace the five straws after the manner shown below, the coin forming a sort of wedge, locking all together. They may then be lifted by the end of one straw as required by the puzzle.

The Two Dogs (page 67). Add lines as shown dotted in the drawing below, and turn the picture partially round, so that what was originally its side is now its top. The dogs will not appear not only to be alive, but to be running at full speed.

The Penetrative Coin (page 67). Fold the paper exactly across the middle of the hole; then take it in both hands, and ask someone

to drop the quarter into the fold. Let it rest just over the hole, its lower edge projecting below. Bend the corners of the paper slightly upwards, as indicated in the drawing. This elongates the opening, and the quarter will fall through by force of its own weight. The paper remains uninjured.

The Fragmented Treasure (page 68). See the drawing below for the proper arrangement of the cards. The position of the letters shows which way the original *top* of each card is to be turned.

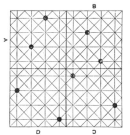

The Two Corks (page 70). The secret lies in the position of the hands as they are brought together. The uninitiated brings them together with the palms of both turned towards the body, with the consequence we have described. To solve the puzzle, turn the palm of the *right hand inward,* and that of the *left hand outward,* in the act of seizing the

corks. They will then not get in each other's way, but may be separated without the least difficulty.

The Balanced Pencil (page 71). Stick the blade of the penknife (which should be a small and light one) into the pencil near the point, in the direction of its longer axis. Then partially close the knife. The precise angle must be ascertained by experiment, as it will vary with the length and weight of the two articles. When you have discovered it, the pencil may be balanced, as shown below, on the tip of the finger.

The Knotted Handkerchief (page 71). The secret lies in the manner of taking hold of the handkerchief. This is laid, twisted ropewise, in a straight line upon the table. The performer then folds his arms, the fingers of the right hand coming out *above* the biceps of the *left* arm, the fingers of the left hand being

passed *below* the biceps of the *right* arm. With the arms still in this position, he bends forward and picks up the handkerchief, the right hand seizing the end lying to the left, and the left hand that which lies to the right. On drawing the arms apart, a knot is formed in the middle of the handkerchief.

The "Forty-Five" Puzzle (page 72). The first of the required numbers is 8. The second is 12. The third is 5. The fourth is 20.

$$8 + 2 = 10$$
$$12 - 2 = 10$$
$$5 \times 2 = 10$$
$$20 \div 2 = 10$$

$$8 + 12 + 5 + 20 = 45$$

The "Twenty-Six" Puzzle (page 73). We append two possible solutions.

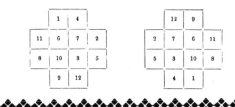

A Singular Subtraction (page 74). This is somewhat of a "quibble." The number 45 is the sum of the digits 1, 2, 3, 4, 5, 6, 7, 8, 9. The puzzle is solved by arranging these in reverse order, and subtracting the original series from them, when the remainder will be found to consist of the same digits in a different order, and therefore making the same sum—45.

$$987654321 = 45$$
$$\underline{123456789 = 45}$$
$$864197532 = 45$$

An Unmanageable Legacy (page 74). The lawyer had a horse of his own, which he drove into the stable with the rest. "Now," he said to John, "take your half." John took nine horses accordingly. James and William were then invited to take their shares, which they did, receiving six and two horses respectively. This division exactly disposed of the seventeen horses of the testator; and the lawyer, pocketing his fee, drove his own steed home again.

The above solution rests on the fact that the sum of the three fractions named, $\frac{1}{2}$, $\frac{1}{3}$, and $\frac{1}{9}$, when reduced to a common denominator, will be found not to amount to unity, but only to $\frac{17}{18}$. The addition of another horse ($=\frac{1}{18}$), bringing the total number up to eighteen, renders it divisible by such common denominator, and enables each to get his proper share, the lawyer then resuming his own $\frac{1}{18}$, which he had lent for the purpose of the division.

A Novel Century (page 75). $9 \times 8 + 7 + 6 + 5 + 4 + 3 + 2 + 1 = 100$.

Another Century (page 75). There are several ways of fulfilling the conditions of the puzzle. The first takes the form of a sum in addition:

$$
\begin{array}{r}
15 \\
36 \\
47 \\
\hline
98 \\
2 \\
\hline
100
\end{array}
$$

Another solution is:

$$1\tfrac{3}{6} + 98\tfrac{27}{54} = 100$$

The Three Legacies (page 75). As the amount of each share is to correspond with length of service, it is plain that the housemaid will receive one share, the parlormaid three, and the cook six—in all, ten shares. The value of a single share is therefore one-tenth of £70, or £7, which is the portion of the housemaid, the parlormaid receiving £21 and the cook £42.

The Magic Cards (page 76). The seven cards are drawn up on a mathematical principle, in such manner that *the first numbers of those in which a given number appears*, when added together, indicate that number.

Suppose, for instance, that the chosen number is 63. This appears in cards I, II, III, IV, V, and VI. The key numbers of these are 1, 2, 4, 8, 16, and 32; and $1 + 2 + 4 + 8 + 16 + 32 = 63$.

If the number 7 were selected, this appears only in cards I, II, and III, whose key numbers are 1, 2, and $4 = 7$.

The principle of construction seems at first sight rather mysterious, but it is simple enough when explained. The reader will note, in the first place, that the first or "key" numbers of each card form a geometrical progression, being 1, 2, 4, 8, 16, 32, 64. The total of these is 127, which is accordingly the highest number included.

It is further to be noted that by appropriate combinations of the above figures *any* total, from 1 up to 127, can be produced.

The first card consists of odd numbers from 1 to 127 inclusive. The second, commencing with 2 (the second term of the geometrical series), consists of alternate groups of two consecutive figures—2, 3; 6, 7; 10, 11; and so on. The third, beginning with 4, the third term of the series, consists of alternate groups of *four* figures—4, 5, 6, 7; 12, 13, 14, 15; 20, 21, 22, 23; and so on. The fourth, commencing with 8, consists in like manner of alternate groups of *eight* figures. The fifth, commencing with 16, of alternate groups of *sixteen* figures. The sixth, commencing with 32, of alternate groups of *thirty-two* figures; and the last, commencing with 64, of a single group, being those from 64 to 127 inclusive.

It will be found that any given number of cards arranged on this principle will produce the desired result, limited by the extent of the geometrical series constituting the first numbers.

The Captives in the Tower (page 78). The boy descended first, using the cannonball as a counterpoise. The queen and her daughter then took the cannonball out of the upper basket, and the daughter descended, the boy acting as counterpoise. The cannonball was then allowed to run down alone. When it reached the ground, the daughter got into the basket along with the cannonball, and their joint weight acted as counterpoise while the queen descended. The princess got out, and the cannonball was sent down alone. The boy then went down, the cannonball ascending. The daughter removed the cannonball and went down alone, her brother ascending. The latter than put the cannonball in the opposite basket, and lowered himself to the ground.

The Two Travellers (page 79). *A*, in his 2½ hours' start, has travelled 10 miles. As *B* gains on him at the rate of a mile an hour, it will take him ten hours to recover this distance, by which time *A* will have been travelling 12½ hours, and will be 50 miles from the point whence he started.

The Wolf, the Goat, and the Cabbages (page 79). This is a very simple problem. It is solved as follows:

1. The boatman first takes across the goat, and leaves him on the opposite side. 2. He returns and fetches the wolf, leaves him on the opposite side, and takes back the goat with him. 3. He leaves the goat at the starting-point, and takes over the basket of cabbages. 4. He leaves the cabbages with the wolf, and returning, fetches the goat.

Or, 1. He takes over the goat. 2. He returns and fetches the cabbages. 3. He takes back the goat, leaves him at the starting-point, and fetches the wolf. 4. He leaves the wolf on the opposite side with the basket of cabbages, and goes back to fetch the goat.

Can You Name It? (page 79). Answer, 20.

$$50 - 20 = 30.$$
$$80 - 50 = 30.$$

A Curious Number (page 80). This problem seems at first sight somewhat formidable, but it is in reality very easy.

Various answers will make it equally correct, according to the value assigned to the smallest part. Thus, if the smallest part is 1, the number will be

$$1 + 40 + 400 + 500 = 941$$

If such unit be 2, the number will be

$$2 + 80 + 800 + 1000 = 1882$$

and so on, *ad infinitum.*

Eleven Guests in Ten Beds (page 80). The fallacy lies in the fact that the real eleventh man remains unprovided with a resting-place. The tenth man having taken possession of the ninth bed, the eleventh man should in due course occupy the tenth bed, but he does not do so. The man who is called from sleeping double in the first bed to occupy this is not the eleventh, but the second, and the real eleventh man goes bedless.

ABOUT THE AUTHOR

Charles Barry Townsend has been writing books on puzzles, games, and magic for over 19 years. He is the author of 16 books, including *The World's Best Puzzles, The World's Most Challenging Puzzles, The World's Toughest Puzzles, The World's Most Baffling Puzzles, The World's Hardest Puzzles, The World's Greatest Puzzles, The World's Most Amazing Puzzles,* and *The World's Best Magic Tricks,* all published by Sterling. Mr. Townsend lives in Mill Creek, Washington, where he spends a good deal of his time thinking up ways to confound and entertain readers like you.

Using the magic mirror cabinet that once belonged to the famous—or infamous—Count Alessandro di Cagliostro, Mr. Townsend has conjured up the likeness of Professor Hoffmann, author of the wonderful problems in this book. Mr. Townsend's dog, Jackie, takes this feat in stride.

Index